FERRARI
458 ITALIA

BY CALVIN CRUZ

BELLWETHER MEDIA • MINNEAPOLIS, MN

™

Are you ready to take it to the extreme?
Torque books thrust you into the action-packed world
of sports, vehicles, mystery, and adventure. These books
may include dirt, smoke, fire, and dangerous stunts.
WARNING: read at your own risk.

This edition first published in 2016 by Bellwether Media, Inc.

No part of this publication may be reproduced in whole or in part without written permission of the publisher.
For information regarding permission, write to Bellwether Media, Inc., Attention: Permissions Department,
5357 Penn Avenue South, Minneapolis, MN 55419.

Library of Congress Cataloging-in-Publication Data

Cruz, Calvin, author.
  Ferrari 458 Italia / by Calvin Cruz.
    pages cm -- (Torque. Car crazy)
  Summary: "Engaging images accompany information about the Ferrari 458 Italia. The combination
of high-interest subject matter and light text is intended for students in grades 3 through 7"--Provided by
publisher.
  Includes bibliographical references and index.
  Audience: Ages 7-12.
  Audience: Grades 3-7.
  ISBN 978-1-62617-282-1 (hardcover : alk. paper)
  1. Ferrari automobile--Juvenile literature. I. Title.
  TL215.F47C785 2016
  629.222'2--dc23
                              2015009715

Printed in the United States of America, North Mankato, MN.

TABLE OF CONTENTS

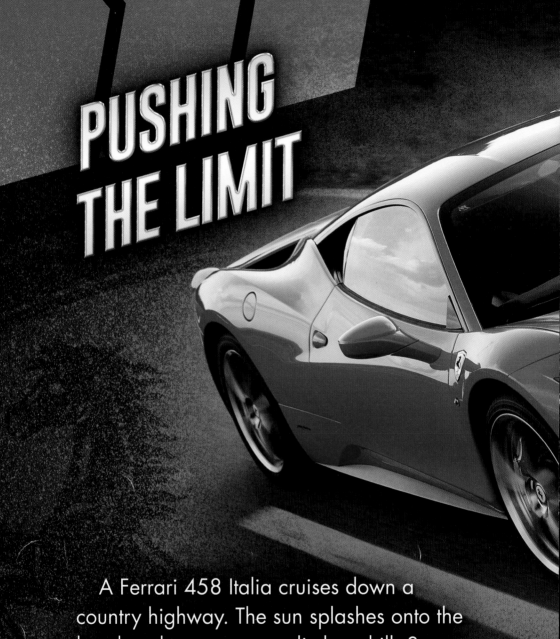

PUSHING THE LIMIT

A Ferrari 458 Italia cruises down a country highway. The sun splashes onto the hood as the **supercar** climbs a hill. Soon, the driver turns onto another road. It has been closed to other cars so the driver can test his car's speed. He steps on the pedal and the 458 Italia takes off.

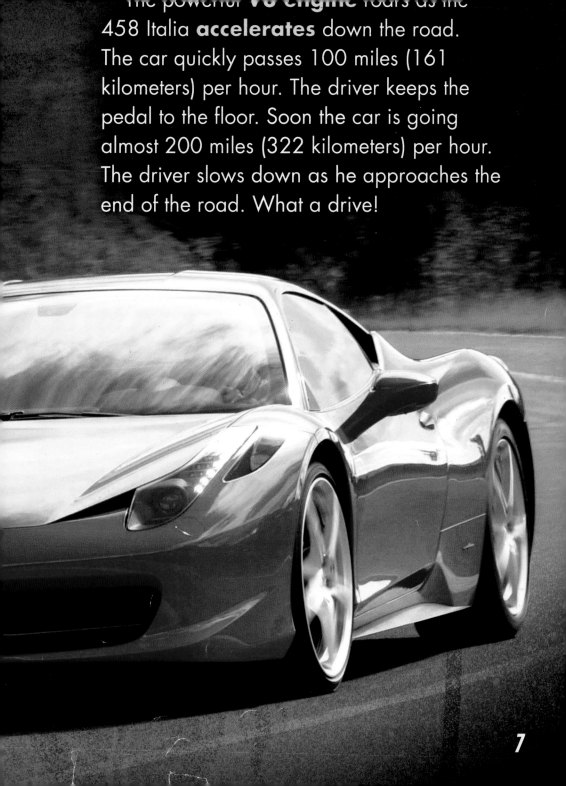

The powerful **V8 engine** roars as the 458 Italia **accelerates** down the road. The car quickly passes 100 miles (161 kilometers) per hour. The driver keeps the pedal to the floor. Soon the car is going almost 200 miles (322 kilometers) per hour. The driver slows down as he approaches the end of the road. What a drive!

THE HISTORY OF FERRARI

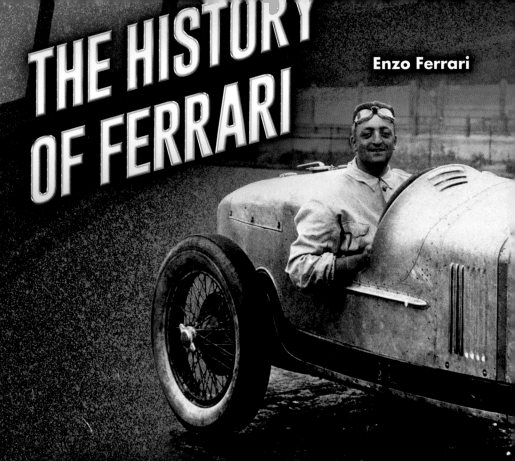

Enzo Ferrari

Enzo Ferrari began racing cars in 1919. For many years, he had success as a driver. By 1929, Enzo had started his own racing team. He spent the next ten years building race cars.

In 1939, he decided to start his own car company. However, Enzo could not build cars during World War II. After the war, he continued working on his designs. By 1947, the first Ferrari car was available to the public.

1947 Ferrari 125 S

Enzo's cars performed well in races. Ferrari's racing victories made the cars grow more popular in the 1950s and 1960s. By 1969, Enzo could not keep up with the demand for his cars. He sold part of the company to the Fiat Group.

Enzo Ferrari in 1965

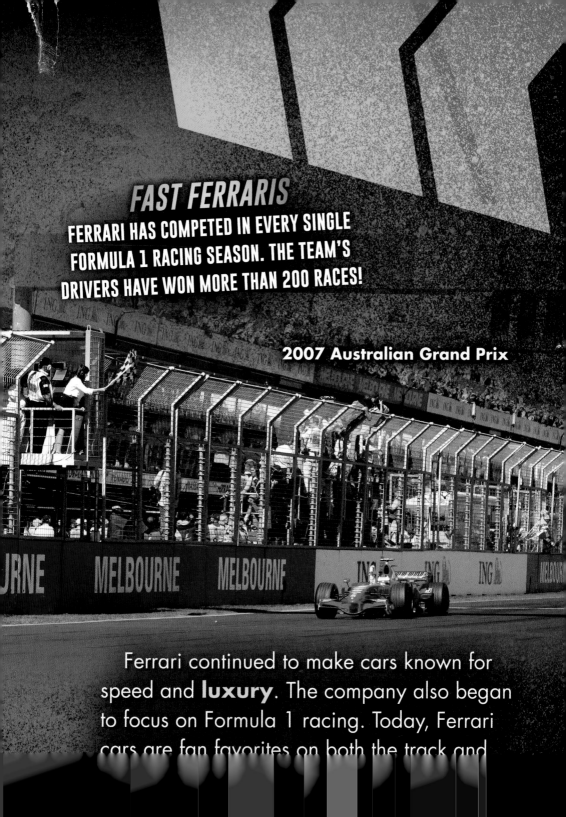

FAST FERRARIS

FERRARI HAS COMPETED IN EVERY SINGLE FORMULA 1 RACING SEASON. THE TEAM'S DRIVERS HAVE WON MORE THAN 200 RACES!

2007 Australian Grand Prix

Ferrari continued to make cars known for speed and **luxury**. The company also began to focus on Formula 1 racing. Today, Ferrari cars are fan favorites on both the track and

FERRARI 458 ITALIA

The 458 Italia was first shown off in 2009. This **coupe** replaced Ferrari's older F430 **model**. The 458's powerful engine and light weight excited sports car fans.

Ferrari F430

ON THE BIG SCREEN

A FERRARI 458 ITALIA NAMED "DINO" APPEARED IN THE MOVIE *TRANSFORMERS: DARK OF THE MOON.*

TECHNOLOGY AND GEAR

The 458 Italia's **interior** is made to feel like a Formula 1 car. A **bucket seat** supports the driver at high speeds. Most of the car's controls are on the steering wheel.

The engine starts with the push of a button. **Paddle shifters** help the driver change gears without moving a hand. Screens behind the steering wheel track the car's performance.

paddle shifter

AN EXPERT'S HELP

FORMULA 1 DRIVER MICHAEL SCHUMACHER HELPED DESIGN THE 458 ITALIA'S INTERIOR. HE WON FIVE STRAIGHT WORLD CHAMPIONSHIPS WITH FERRARI'S TEAM IN THE EARLY 2000s.

Michael Schumacher

Traction control settings help the 458 Italia grip the road in all conditions. With the flick of a switch, the driver can change the car's performance to fit different road surfaces.

The 458 Italia's engine sits behind the driver's seat. The car's trunk space is in the front end.

4.5L V8 engine

Much of the 458 Italia is made of **aluminum**. This metal keeps the car light but strong. The car's body sits low to the ground. This helps the tires grip the road at high speeds.

Powerful brakes help the driver stay in control. The 458 Italia can go from 62 miles (100 kilometers) per hour to a complete stop in only 106.6 feet (32.5 meters)!

A POWERFUL NAME

THE NUMBER IN THE ITALIA'S NAME COMES FROM ITS POWER. "458" COMBINES THE NUMBERS FROM ITS 4.5L V8 ENGINE.

2015 FERRARI 458 ITALIA SPECIFICATIONS

CAR STYLE	COUPE OR SPIDER (CONVERTIBLE)
ENGINE	4.5L V8 ENGINE
TOP SPEED	201 MILES (323 KILOMETERS) PER HOUR
0 - 60 TIME	ABOUT 3.30 SECONDS
HORSEPOWER	562 HP (419 KILOWATTS) @ 9000 RPM
DRY WEIGHT	3,042 POUNDS (1,380 KILOGRAMS)
WIDTH	76.3 INCHES (194 CENTIMETERS)
LENGTH	178.2 INCHES (453 CENTIMETERS)
HEIGHT	47.8 INCHES (121 CENTIMETERS)
WHEEL SIZE	20 INCHES (51 CENTIMETERS)
COST	STARTS AT $240,000

TODAY AND THE FUTURE

The 458 Italia continues to be a favorite among Ferrari fans. It has won more than 30 awards since it came out in 2009. However, Ferrari recently announced that the 458 Italia is being replaced by a new model. The 488 GTB has a lot to live up to!

Ferrari 488 GTB

TAPERED WINDOW LINE

FRONT AIR VENT

SLANTED HEADLIGHTS

Ferrari 458 Spider (Italia convertible)

NOT JUST RED

WHEN CAR RACING BEGAN, ALL ITALIAN CARS WERE RED. NOW BUYERS CAN CHOOSE FROM MANY COLORS!

GLOSSARY

accelerates—increases in speed

aluminum—a strong, lightweight metal

bucket seat—a seat with a rounded back to keep a person in place when turning at high speeds

coupe—a car with a hard roof and two doors

interior—the inside of a car

luxury—expensive and offering great comfort

model—a specific kind of car

paddle shifters—paddles on the steering wheel of a car that allow a driver to change gears

supercar—an expensive and high-performing sports car

traction control—a system that helps cars grip the road in different conditions

V8 engine—an engine with 8 cylinders arranged in the shape of a "V"

TO LEARN MORE

AT THE LIBRARY

Aloian, Molly. *Ferrari*. New York, N.Y.: Crabtree Pub., 2011.

Power, Bob. *Ferraris.* New York, N.Y.: Gareth Stevens Pub., 2012.

Quinlan, Julia J. *Ferrari*. New York, N.Y.: PowerKids Press, 2013.

ON THE WEB

Learning more about the Ferrari 458 Italia is as easy as 1, 2, 3.

1. Go to www.factsurfer.com.

2. Enter "Ferrari 458 Italia" into the search box.

3. Click the "Surf" button and you will see a list of related web sites.

With factsurfer.com, finding more information is just a click away.

INDEX

The images in this book are reproduced through the courtesy of: Matthew Richardson/ Alamy, front cover, pp. 6-7, 13 (top); Fiat Chrysler Automobiles, pp. 4-5, 14, 18, 21 (bottom); Magic Car Pics/ Rex/ REX USA, pp. 5, 6, 19; Bettmann/ Corbis, pp. 8-9; Allstar Picture Library/ Alamy, p. 9; Manuel Litran/ Corbis, p. 10; Roland Weihrauch/ dpa/ Corbis, p. 11; Chad Horwedel, p. 12; Bellwether Media, p. 13 (bottom); Ben Radford/ Getty Images, p. 15; Terry Foster/ Alamy, p. 16; WENN Ltd/ Alamy, p. 17 (bottom); VanderWolf Images, p. 20; Max Earey, p. 21 (top left, top right); Faiz Zaki, p. 21 (top center).